Praise for
Shine!
Radiating the Love of God

"Is there a young woman aged 13-18 in your life? Then have I got a Bible study for you! *Shine! Radiating the Love of God* is one of the best resources I've seen for this age group. This nine-week Bible study is fun, and it addresses real life issues such as friendship, modesty, guys, technology, and much more. Shine the light of God into your teens and watch His light radiate through them. I highly recommend this book!"

~ MICHELLE COX, CO-AUTHOR OF *WHEN CALLS THE HEART* DEVOTIONALS
AUTHOR OF *JUST 18 SUMMERS* AND CREATOR/DEVELOPER OF THE *JUST 18 SUMMERS*® BRAND OF PARENTING PRODUCTS AND RESOURCES

"Yes! Everything I want my daughter to know about the teen years is right here in one place: *Shine! Radiating the Love of God*, by Deborah Presnell. As I read this study for teen leaders or mothers and daughters, I become convinced that this is the very scriptural teaching young teens need to hear today as they face the challenges of growing up while still remaining close to the Lord. Deborah shares from her own experiences and her rich study of the Word. This is truly an inspired work by a truly inspiring teacher and speaker. I highly recommend it for all mothers of teenage daughters."

~ ANN TATLOCK, AWARD-WINNING AUTHOR

"I love the way Deborah gives confidence to teens, enabling them to feel loved, and lovely, and precious to God. They will want to respond with the best that's in them, not because He 'demands' it but because of love. So encouraging, inspiring!"

~ YVONNE LEHMAN, AWARD-WINNING AUTHOR

"Having just exited my teen years and knowing that *Shine! Radiating the Light of God* is coming out makes me smile. I wish I'd had this Bible study when I was going through the changes and trials of teen life. Debbie Presnell is not only a woman who writes about radiating the love of Christ, she lives it! This study will transform this generation and ignite fires within the hearts of teenage girls everywhere so they are equipped to shine brightly in their schools, homes, churches, and communities.

~ EMMA DANZEY | CHRISTIAN ARTIST

"Mrs. Presnell's Bible study has helped me to keep in mind the important things — number one, God! But she also taught me about friends, boys, and modesty. She helped me learn what my true friends do to show that they are really true friends. She taught me how God wants me to behave and what qualities to look for in boys. Her study made me open up and make personal connections. I'll always be thankful for her teaching me this Bible study."

~ Katie, 9th grade participant

"It's scary being a mom in this day and age. So I was very grateful the summer before my oldest daughter, Emily, was to enter high school. She had the opportunity to participate in *Shine! Radiating the Love of God* taught by Deborah Presnell. Deborah's Bible study for young women helped open the dialogue between me and my daughter, covering a wide variety of topics such as how to dress, gossip, choosing friends, boys and sex. For any mom who has that occasional doubt as to whether you're doing a good job raising your children, *Shine! Radiating the Love of God* is a must! Bring in the reinforcements…I have two more daughters who are heading for high school!"

~ Lori Marett, Wife, Mother of three daughters, Screenwriter, Director of the *Gideon Media Arts Conference and Film Festival*

Shine! Radiating the Love of God is a must for teen girls everywhere. The teen world is full of struggles, drama and questions — and this Bible study addresses these issues and helps prepare girls for the world we live in today. Following God's path during the teen years can be challenging, but the road is made easier through this insightful study on how to be godly women in a world that doesn't always view being a believer as a popular decision. I hope young women everywhere have the opportunity to do this study and take it to heart — ultimately standing out and shining for God.

~ Jan Westmark, Author, co-founder of Shine! Ministries, and Editor-In-Chief of *Sidelines* Magazine

"This Bible study has been so amazing and helpful to me. I am not afraid about school drama after this. This study showed me how to find true and trustworthy friends, and how to balance out my time. The chapter on 'boys' was the most helpful. It really put it in perspective on what to look for and what not to tolerate. I love this Bible study! Thank you so much!"

~ Julianne, 9th grade participant

Shine!

Shine!

Radiating the Love of God

A Bible Study

Designed for Young Women in Middle School and High School

Deborah Presnell

Broken Arrow, OK

Unless otherwise indicated, Scripture quotations in this book are taken from *The Study Bible, New International Version*. Copyright ©1986, 1992, 1996 by The Zondervan Corporation, and from the *New International Version* online (NIV). Used by permission.

Scripture quotations marked ESV are taken from *The Holy Bible, English Standard Version*. Copyright © 2001 by Crossway Bibles, a division of Good News Publishers.

Scripture quotations marked HCSB are taken from *Holman Christian Standard Bible*. Copyright © 1999, 2000, 2002, 2003, 2009 by Holman Bible Publishers, Nashville Tennessee. All rights reserved.

Scripture quotations marked NASB are taken from the *New American Standard Bible*. Copyright © 1960, 1962, 1963, 1968, 1971, 1972, 1973, 1975, 1977, 1995 by The Lockman Foundation.

Scripture quotations marked NKJV taken from the *New King James Version*®. Copyright © 1982 by Thomas Nelson. Used by permission. All rights reserved.

Scripture quotations marked NLT are taken from *New Living Translation*. Copyright © 1996, 2004, 2007, 2013 by Tyndale House Foundation. Used by permission of Tyndale House Publishers Inc., Carol Stream, Illinois. All rights reserved.

With the exception of brief quotations embodied in a review, this book or parts thereof may not be reproduced in any form without permission. Photocopying, scanning, uploading, and/or distribution of this book via the Internet or any other means without written permission of the publisher is illegal.

For Information Contact
Grace Publishing
PO Box 1233
Broken Arrow, OK 74013

Cover Image: Depositphotos

ISBN 13: 978-1-60495-014-4

Copyright © 2015 by Deborah Presnell. Published by Grace Publishing House, Broken Arrow, Oklahoma. All rights reserved.

About Copyrights

First Timothy 5:17-18 instructs us to give the laborer his wages, specifically those who labor in the Word and doctrine. Even so, some people who would never shoplift may think nothing of copying a book. The results are the same; it's theft.

As Christians, we have a moral, as well as a legal, responsibility to see that authors receive fair compensation for their efforts. Many of them depend on the income from the sale of their books as their livelihood, as do the artists, editors, and numerous other people who work to make their books available to you.

With the exception of brief quotations embodied in a review, this book, or parts thereof may not be reproduced in any form without permission. It is protected by copyright and is not intended to be shared with or duplicated by others who have not purchased it for themselves from authorized sellers. Photocopying, scanning, uploading, and/or distribution of this book via the Internet or any other means without written permission of the publisher is illegal and punishable by law.

If you have a copy of this book that was not purchased by or for you, please be aware that you are using an illegal, pirated copy. Please purchase only authorized editions, from authorized sellers, and do not participate in or encourage piracy of copyrighted materials.

Your support of the author's rights is appreciated.

Dedication

*T*o my daughter, Julianne Grace

I vividly remember that day when you and I were sitting on your bed and I said, "I hope you are prepared to handle all the drama that teens face. I wish I could gather your friends together and teach all of you how to handle the problems you will face."

You said, "Let's do it!" So we did. And every Friday night for nine weeks throughout the summer, we gathered together to study God's Word.

May you shine for Jesus all the days of your life!

Acknowledgements

*F*irst and foremost, I want to thank God for providing the amazingly beautiful Scriptures. His Word is the roadmap for our lives — the compass that takes us where He wants us to go. Thank you, God, for the privilege of raising daughters.

I also want to extend a special word of thanks to Yvonne Lehman, Ann Tatlock, Michelle Cox, Deborah Harvey, Lori Marret, Beth Barker, Carolyn Clark, Constance Wright, Diana Flegal, Jan Westmark, and Emma Danzey Burnham for their support, expert editing suggestions, and encouragement. I am so grateful!

Thank you, Alan, for giving me the time and encouragement to work on this project and for believing in me. I am blessed to have you as my husband.

Finally, I am so grateful to Terri Kalfas at Grace Publishing for believing in me. Thank you for your encouragement and support and for taking a chance on me. I am so excited to be working with you!

Contents

Let's Get Started 13

Chapter 1 *I Am a Treasure* 15

Chapter 2 *Radiant Fashion* 23

Chapter 3 *Brilliant Beauty* 33

Chapter 4 *No-Regrets Dating* 41

Chapter 5 *Sparkle!* 53

Chapter 6 *Fabulous Friendship* 63

Chapter 7 *Rising Above the Darkness* 71

Chapter 8 *I've Got Talent* 83

Chapter 9 *Glitter!* 93

Recommended Devotionals 102

End Notes 103

Notes for Facilitator / Parent / Teacher 105

About the Author 119

Let's Get Started!

The issues you face today are not really new problems. On some level, they are the same problems women have faced since the beginning of time — feeling accepted, gossip, Satan's lies, guys, and the overwhelming stress that accompanies each of those. The difference is, today's technology enables that which was once hidden, to be exposed.

What pictures come to mind when you hear the word *dark*?

_____

_____

What do you think of when you hear the word *light*?

_____

_____

Jesus said, *"I have come into the world as a light, so that no one who believes in Me should stay in darkness."* (John 12:46) Our mission as found in Matthew 5:16 is this: *Let your light shine before men in such a way that they may see your good works, and glorify your Father who is in heaven.* (NASB)

Before we can be *light* to others we need to be certain we have the truth. For starters ask yourself:

Do I know what God thinks about me?	YES	NO
Do I believe what God thinks about me?	YES	NO
Do I think about how other people view me?	YES	NO
Do I wonder if my friends really like me?	YES	NO

You are not alone.

At the end of Chapter 1 you will list the names of your friends joining you in Bible study. Take a few minutes as a group and discuss what you hope to get out of this study. If you are comfortable, share with the group something you would like to pray about. Record each group member's prayer requests. Commit to pray for each other throughout the week. At your next meeting, discuss updates and answers. Discuss how sometimes God says "No" or "Wait," but He will always do what is best for you.

Now, let's press on to Chapter 1 and discover who you really are.

Chapter 1

I Am a Treasure

God, who said, "Let there be light in the darkness," has made this light shine in our hearts so we could know the glory of God that is seen in the face of Jesus Christ.

2 Corinthians 4:6 NLT

Seeing yourself through God's eyes is the beginning of complete truth. His love for you remains the same, no matter your behavior. Your conduct will either displease Him or bring Him delight but it will never remove His love. John 1:12 confirms you are a child of God. You're not *what* you do; you're *who* you are! You're God's child, and as such your identity is in Christ!

Satan, however, is the Deceiver and Prince of Darkness. His lies attack our emotions and our self-worth. Recent studies on teenagers and self-esteem reveal the following:

- "Over 70 percent of girls age 15 to 17 avoid normal daily activities, such as attending school, when they feel bad about their looks.
- Seventy-five percent of girls with low self-esteem reported engaging in negative activities like cutting, bullying, smoking, drinking, or eating disorders. This compares to 25 percent of girls with high self-esteem.
- Teen girls who have a negative view of themselves are four times more likely to take part in activities with boys that they've ended up regretting later." [1]

Do you know girls who fit these descriptions? What about you? Do you feel inadequate, incompetent or not accepted? Write your thoughts on the lines provided.

_____

_____

Many teenagers admit they base their identity on how others view them. But here's the truth. God views you as acceptable already. God not only accepts you but He uniquely designed you — from the color of your eyes to each perfectly placed freckle.

Read the following Scriptures and draw a line to the verse that matches them to how God feels about you. Then personalize God's message by writing your name on the blank line in the scripture. You don't have to have the exact translation of the reference provided. You can get the gist of the verse from any translation.

Jeremiah 1:5	*He who touches _____, touches the Apple of My Eye.*
Jeremiah 29:11	*If you obey Me fully and keep My covenant, then out of all Nations you, _____ will be my treasured possession. Although the whole earth is Mine.*
Zechariah 2:8b (ESV)	*Before I formed you in the womb I knew you, _____, before you were born I set you apart; I anointed you as a prophet to the nations.*
Exodus 19:5	*You formed my inward parts; You knitted me together in my mother's womb. I praise You, For I, _____, am fearfully and wonderfully made.*
Psalm 139:13-14a (ESV)	*Yes, I have loved you with an everlasting love; Therefore with lovingkindness I have drawn _____.*
Ephesians 2:10 (ESV)	*In every nation, anyone (including you) _____ who fears Him and does what is right is acceptable to Him.*
Isaiah 43:1b	*_____ is His workmanship, created in Christ Jesus for good works, which God prepared beforehand, that we should walk in them.*
Jeremiah 31:3 (NKJV)	*I know the plans I have for you, _____, declares the LORD, plans to prosper you and not to harm you, plans to give you hope and a future.*
Acts 10:35 (ESV)	*Do not fear, for I redeemed you; I have summoned you by name, _____ ; You are mine.*

Zechariah 2:8 tells us God uses the phrase "the apple of His eye" to describe His people.

The apple, or pupil, is considered the most delicate part of the eye. When we look into another person's eyes, we see our own reflection. Similarly, when God looks into our eyes, He sees His reflection.

We're made in the image of Christ. Everything in creation shows how beautiful God is. Because we're made in His image, we're beautiful.

We're precious, cherished and beloved.

What do you think *workmanship* means? _____

_____

_____

That's right! You are a work of art, a masterpiece, a finished product. Did you know you were this special and precious to God? Based on the previous scriptures, what do you conclude about God's view of you and your worth?

_____

_____

The devil sends a contrary (opposite) message. Read John 10:10. What three things does the thief attempt to do?

_____   _____   _____

Steal the truth. Kill your self-worth. Destroy the light. How does the Deceiver use the media to destroy your self-worth? _____

_____

_____

See it for the lie that it is. Satan can't have your soul but He will try to ruin your life by filling you with fear, inadequacies, worthlessness, and shame, preventing you from having a life filled with purpose.

While Satan tries to make our life as uncomfortable as possible, God wants us to enjoy everything He has created. One of His amazing creations is the beach. We comb the sand for shells, swim, or enjoy the sunrise blending red, orange, and yellow across the early-morning sky. God says something about the beach too. Read Psalm 139:17-18 and fill in the missing word:

How precious are Your thoughts about me, O God, How great is the sum of them! If I should count them, they would be more in number than the _____ .

Scientist Robert Krulwich reports, "If you assume a grain of sand has an average size, and you calculate how many grains are in a teaspoon and then multiply by all the beaches and deserts in the world, the Earth has roughly (and we're speaking very roughly here) 7.5×10^{18} grains of sand, or seven quintillion, five hundred quadrillion grains."[2]

I can't even write that number. The point is, when God says His thoughts about us are more numerous than the sand on the beaches, He's declaring He thinks about us a whole lot. The thought is unfathomable. But try to wrap your mind around that fact for a few minutes. Do you believe God cares about you and you are never out of His thoughts?

     YES   No   NOT SURE

If your answer is NO or NOT SURE, ask God to help you believe.

In whom do you place your identity? _____ !

When the world and the Prince of Darkness tell you that you don't matter, remember God's truth says you do. No one can take God's absolute truth away from you. No one can steal your true identity. Believe God when He says you are His treasured possession, you have a purpose, you were perfectly designed, and you are completely acceptable. Place your identity in Christ — this will enable you to confidently light up your school and community with the truth of God!

Praying for Yourself and Others

Never stop praying

1 Thessalonians 5:17 NLT

Share with the group something you would like to pray about. Record each group member's prayer requests below. Commit to pray for each other throughout the week.

Friends	Prayer Requests

Journaling and Doodling Your Thoughts and Feelings

What part of this study meant the most to you? What do you think God is teaching you? Are you having a hard time understanding any part? Ask God to help you believe. Lines are provided for you to write your thoughts, but you can also use the space below the lines to draw a picture or illustrate your feelings. In chapters 2, 4, 5, 7, 8 and 9 you will have an entire page for each.

_____

_____

_____

_____

_____

_____

_____

Optional Activities

1. **Treasure Ring** — Using small, colorful index cards, rewrite the verses containing your name with colorful markers. If you choose, decorate each card with stickers. Then, using a hole puncher, punch a hole at the top left corner of each card. Use a medal ring to hold the cards together. Carry these cards with you wherever you go, and refer to them often!

2. **Sand Bag** — Using 2 x 3 inch clear-plastic jewelry bags purchased from a craft store, and a bag of children's play sand, scoop a bit of sand into a bag. Seal the bag shut. On a tiny piece of blue paper write "God constantly thinks about me. Psalm 139:17-18a." Staple this note to the bag. Keep the bag on your vanity or nightstand as a visual reminder of God's love.

3. **Love Myself Alphabet** — Write the letters of the alphabet vertically on a sheet of paper. Beside each letter, write a word that describes you. For example, A = Adorable, B = Bubbly, C = Creative, etc.

4. **Sing Along** — to Chris Tomlin's *Jesus Loves Me*.

Spending Time Alone with God

Monday: Isaiah 43:18-19

Forget the former things; do not dwell on the past. See, I am doing a new thing! Now it springs up; do you not perceive it? I am making a way in the wilderness and streams in the wasteland.

Tuesday: Philippians 4:8

Whatever is true, whatever is noble, whatever is right, whatever is pure, whatever is lovely, whatever is admirable — if anything is excellent or praiseworthy — think about such things.

Wednesday: Galatians 5:22-26

The fruit of the Spirit is love, joy, peace, forbearance, kindness, goodness, faithfulness, gentleness and self-control. Against such things there is no law. Those who belong to Christ Jesus have crucified the flesh with its passions and desires. Since we live by the Spirit, let us keep in step with the Spirit. Let us not become conceited, provoking and envying each other.

Thursday: Psalm 37:4-8

Take delight in the Lord, and he will give you the desires of your heart. Commit your way to the Lord; trust in him and he will do this: He will make your righteous reward shine like the dawn, your vindication like the noonday sun. Be still before the Lord and wait patiently for him; do not fret when people succeed in their ways, when they carry out their wicked schemes. Refrain from anger and turn from wrath; do not fret — it leads only to evil.

Friday: John 15:1-8

I am the true vine, and my Father is the gardener. He cuts off every branch in me that bears no fruit, while every branch that does bear fruit he prunes so that it will be even more fruitful. You are already clean because of the word I have spoken to you. Remain in me, as I also remain in you. No branch can bear fruit by itself; it must remain in the vine. Neither can you bear fruit unless you remain in me. I am the vine; you are the branches. If you remain in me and I in you, you will bear much fruit; apart from me you can do nothing. If you do not remain in me, you are like a branch that is thrown away and withers; such branches are picked up, thrown into the fire and burned. If you remain in me and my words remain in you, ask whatever you wish, and it will be done for you. This is to my Father's glory, that you bear much fruit, showing yourselves to be my disciples.

Chapter 2

Radiant Fashion

If you are filled with light, with no dark corners, then your whole life will be radiant, as though a floodlight were filling you with light.

Luke 11:36 NLT

What you choose to wear or how you fix your hair gives you a creative way of expressing yourself. It's also much of the world's primary interest — to look beautiful on the outside and bring attention to ourselves. But as a godly young woman, your physical image also sends a message about what you love and value. What you show externally is a reflection of your inner character and your personal relationship with Jesus Christ. Because our culture does emphasize external beauty, we have countless stores in which to shop, and a variety of styles from which to choose. From athletic wear to jeans and dresses, there is a wide assortment of super cute clothes. Additionally, many stores carry accessories to enhance these styles. Where do you like to shop? What do these stores says about your personal style and preference? How would you define your personal style?

_____

_____

_____

_____

_____

In Proverbs 31:22 the author describes the woman as a fine dresser, indicating she gives thought to what she wears. Contemplate the different styles and colors that look good on you. Maybe you prefer a simple look and style. Maybe having a designer, voguish, chic style, better describes you. Either way is fine and both can be fashionable!

Read and summarize 1 Peter 3:3-4. (NASB) _____

_____

_____

_____

Do you think Peter means you cannot have braids? _____

The Greek word translated in English as *adorn* is *kosmeo*, which is where we get our word *cosmetic*. It means to "make ready."

The following four guidelines will help you make yourself ready.

1. Discretion. Read and summarize Proverbs 11:22 and Proverbs 2:11.

   _____

   _____

   _____

   _____

   How will discretion protect your:

   Reputation _____

   _____

   Witness _____

   _____

   Image _____

   _____

   Dressing indiscreetly is a careless disrespect of your own body. But if your outfit says you respect yourself, others will respect you too.

2. Temptation. Read and summarize 1 Corinthians 10:32.

_____

_____

_____

_____

Guys are visual. They could easily be distracted by your body, and to lust is a sin. Help Christian young men by being careful not to draw attention to parts of your body that were meant for only your future husband to see.

3. Purity. Read and summarize Ephesians 5:3 and Colossians 3:5.

_____

_____

_____

_____

You are called to be sexually pure, and your clothing should not suggest otherwise. Dress like you are preserving your sexual purity.

4. Modesty. Read and summarize 1 Timothy 2:9-10.

_____

_____

_____

_____

The fashion industry exists because of our culture's emphasis on outward beauty. It caters to our desire to focus on our outer beauty. How do you think our culture views the body?

_____

_____

What or who influences how beautiful you look? With whom do you compare yourself? _____

_____

_____

Clothes can enhance your beauty, or take away from it. For example, the color of your shirt can bring out the color of your gorgeous eyes, magnifying their natural beauty. But if your shirt is too low cut, the gaze of the onlooker is automatically drawn to the cleavage or breasts. Your sparkling eyes, smile, or hair, will go unnoticed.

God made you beautifully. You can recognize that God does good work, so don't be shy about this next question. What do you consider attractive about your body? What are your best features? If you find it hard to answer this, ask a friend to tell you.

_____

_____

_____

_____

_____

The problem is not adorning ourselves externally. The problem begins when we allow our external appearance to become our main concern. When our appearance takes top priority, we neglect our inner beauty, which is what lasts forever.

Excessive focus on appearance can lead to unhealthy behaviors and sinful attitudes. Which of these could be potentially harmful side effects to you specifically?

_____ discontentment	_____ selfishness	_____ pride
_____ jealousy	_____ feeling of worthlessness	_____ wasteful spending
_____ depression	_____ discouragement	_____ immodesty

How so? _____

_____

_____

_____

How short is too short, how low is too low, how tight is too tight? Bend over in the mirror so you can see what others will see. Pray. Ask God to teach you what is appropriate.

If you view yourself as worthy, special, adored by God, and made for a purpose, then those attitudes will be reflected in your character and your external appearance.

A Spirit-filled young woman is confident, self-controlled, and treats her body with respect and integrity. Shining the light of God starts on the inside. And glitter lotion and sparkly hair spray can definitely make you shine on the outside too!

Praying for Yourself and Others

Don't worry about anything; instead, pray about everything. Tell God what you need, and thank him for all he has done.

Philippians 4:6 NLT

What are you praying about this week?

_____

_____

_____

_____

_____

_____

_____

_____

_____

_____

_____

_____

_____

_____

_____

_____

Journaling Your Thoughts

What part of this study meant the most to you? What do you think God is teaching you? Are you having a hard time understanding any part? Ask God to help you believe. Write your thoughts.

_____
_____
_____
_____
_____
_____
_____
_____
_____
_____
_____
_____
_____
_____
_____
_____
_____

Doodling Your Thoughts and Feelings

Use this page to draw a picture or illustrate your feelings.

Optional Activities

1. **Fashion Poster** — As a group, look through a variety of magazines and cut out pictures of women dressed in a variety of different outfits. Then glue these pictures to a large poster board. Decide what each outfit says about the person. For example, this woman appears confident and sophisticated as she works. That woman, half dressed, is saying, "Come and get it!"

2. **Fashion Collage** — Using store catalogs, store flyers and magazines, create a personal outfit by cutting out individual pieces of clothing. For example, cut out a cute shirt, jeans, a great pair of shoes, and a purse or other accessories. Glue them to a piece of construction paper. Glue a photo of your face to the outfit. Dressing modestly and fashionably makes you the next top model!

Spending Time Alone with God

Monday: Ephesians 3:16-21

I pray that out of his glorious riches he may strengthen you with power through his Spirit in your inner being, so that Christ may dwell in your hearts through faith. And I pray that you, being rooted and established in love, may have power, together with all the Lord's holy people, to grasp how wide and long and high and deep is the love of Christ, and to know this love that surpasses knowledge — that you may be filled to the measure of all the fullness of God. Now to him who is able to do immeasurably more than all we ask or imagine, according to his power that is at work within us, to him be glory in the church and in Christ Jesus throughout all generations, for ever and ever! Amen

Tuesday: 2 Corinthians 4:16-5:1

We do not lose heart. Though outwardly we are wasting away, yet inwardly we are being renewed day by day. For our light and momentary troubles are achieving for us an eternal glory that far outweighs them all. So we fix our eyes not on what is seen, but on what is unseen, since what is seen is temporary, but what is unseen is eternal. For we know that if the earthly tent we live in is destroyed, we have a building from God, an eternal house in heaven, not built by human hands.

Wednesday: John 15: 11-17

I have told you this so that my joy may be in you and that your joy may be complete. My command is this: Love each other as I have loved you. Greater love has no one than this: to lay down one's life for one's friends. You are my friends if you do what I command. I no longer call you servants, because a servant does not know his master's business. Instead, I have called you friends, for everything that I learned from my Father I have made known to you. You did not choose me, but I chose you and appointed you so that you might go and bear fruit — fruit that will last — and so that whatever you ask in my name the Father will give you. This is my command: Love each other.

Thursday: 2 Corinthians 5:16-17

From now on we regard no one from a worldly point of view. Though we once regarded Christ in this way, we do so no longer. Therefore, if anyone is in Christ, the new creation has come: The old has gone, the new is here!

Friday: Romans 12:1-2

I urge you, brothers and sisters, in view of God's mercy, to offer your bodies as a living sacrifice, holy and pleasing to God — this is your true and proper worship. Do not conform to the pattern of this world, but be transformed by the renewing of your mind. Then you will be able to test and approve what God's will is — his good, pleasing and perfect will.

Chapter 3

Brilliant Beauty

As for me, I shall walk in my integrity.

Psalm 26:11a NASB

Y ou probably know that integrity is something good, but what do you think it means?

It's true that in most situations the first thing other people notice about us is our appearance. Think about a crime scene and a witness for example. "Can you describe the perpetrator?" the policeman asks.

It's human nature to notice others and their appearance. We notice hair, clothes, skin color, height, and other distinctive features. Given a few extra seconds, we might even notice the glitter lotion and shiny hair spray that make them glow…at least externally. Often in a brief episode we judge or label a person as attractive or unattractive. That determination lies within each person's definition of beauty. How would you define beauty? _____

As a Christian young woman, how you decide to adorn yourself is a reflection of your heart, what you believe about your worth, what you value, what you emphasize, and where you focus and place your attention. This has nothing to do with your God-given appearance. This part is your inner beauty.

Inner beauty can be described as *character*. Dictionaries define character as the mental and moral qualities distinctive to an individual. Synonyms include: personality, nature, disposition, temperament, mentality.

How would you describe your personality? What are your most lovable and endearing traits? Is there anything you would change? _____

_____

Think about your closest, most special friends. What draws you to them?

_____

_____

Now think about the people you purposely have chosen to avoid. Maybe it's because they made you feel stupid. Maybe they've embarrassed you, lied to you, or were mean to you. This has nothing to do with how they look, but rather, how they valued you as a person.

People might be attracted to outer beauty at first, but what sustains a relationship is inner beauty.

Let's review 1 Peter 3:3-4. Peter wrote, *"Your adornment must not be merely external — braiding the hair, and wearing gold jewelry, or putting on dresses; but let it be the hidden person of the heart, with the imperishable quality of a gentle and quiet spirit, which is precious in the sight of God."* (NASB)

There's nothing wrong with trying to look our best. Peter is saying that it becomes a problem when our external appearance takes precedence over the development of our inner beauty. During New Testament times women were extravagant in the adornment of hair. It was customary for women to dye their hair and use costly hairpins or even wear blonde wigs with gold threads. Emphasis was placed on hair and outer beauty. Peter didn't say to neglect our personal appearance. He said it shouldn't overshadow our inner beauty.

We need to put as much care and thought toward our inner beauty as we do our outer beauty. Our character defines us. It's our attitude, disposition, thoughts that eventually have the potential to become spoken words.

What do you think having a gentle and quiet spirit means?

_____

_____

The *KJV Dictionary* defines a gentle and quiet spirit as one that is free from disturbance and commotion; is still, tranquil, calm, peaceful, not agitated.[3] A quiet spirit has little to do with how much we talk. Rather, it's that our speech is self-controlled, gentle, filled with grace and knowledge. It means when confrontation or accountability issues arise, we speak from an outpouring of love stemming from a right attitude and pure motivation.

Read Colossians 3:12. What five things are we to put on?

_____

_____

_____

_____

Without the light of Jesus Christ burning within our heart, soul, and mind, we will not be able to portray these traits. These come from God — for He is Light. But with Jesus as our focus, each day these traits can and will become part of us and will become obvious to others. It happens naturally as we spend time with God in prayer and reading His word. He alone transforms our hearts. When He does, our outside becomes beautiful as well.

Now look at Colossians 3:8. What should we "take off" or get rid of?

_____

_____

_____

_____

We need to put aside, anger, wrath, malice, and slander, but let's focus on *filthy words*.

When the filthy words our culture uses become part of our normal conversation, we are not reflecting Jesus Christ. Instead, we are blending in with a dark culture.

God put in each of us the ability to creatively express how we are feeling. Godly wisdom enables us to choose an acceptable vocabulary. Our beautiful attributes are what draw others to see Christ's love. Filthy language does not.

Different translations use different terms for filthy talk: filthy language (NIV), dirty language (NLT), obscene talk (ESV), abusive language (NASB). No matter which translation you like to read, God says don't have a foul mouth. If your talk is filthy, then your heart and mind are filthy, and your inner beauty isn't so beautiful any more. If you have been subjected to this type of language your whole life and it is typical and habitual for you, then ask God to help you change. Matthew 23:26 tells us to cleanse first the inside then the outside will be beautiful.

Read John 14:16-17. The moment we place our faith in Jesus Christ He sends a Helper to dwell within us who is the _____.

Read 1 Corinthians 6:19-20. Our bodies are _____.

Respect and esteem your body. Value it and treat it well. Don't misuse or abuse it. Honoring God with your body glorifies God and points others to Him. Onlookers see your inner qualities and love, and are drawn to you! Therefore they're drawn to Jesus Christ. Emphasis on your inner beauty will make your outer beauty more radiant.

Outer beauty will eventually fade away, but the beauty of a godly woman never fades. Psalm 45:13 tells us *the king's daughter is glorious within.* You are so beautiful!

Praying for Yourself and Others

Jesus told his disciples a story to show that they should always pray and never give up.

Luke 18:1 NLT

What are you praying about this week?

_____
_____
_____
_____
_____
_____
_____
_____
_____
_____
_____
_____
_____
_____
_____
_____
_____
_____

Journaling and Doodling Your Thoughts and Feelings

What part of this study meant the most to you? What do you think God is teaching you? Are you having a hard time understanding any part? Ask God to help you believe. Write your thoughts. You can also use the space below the lines to draw a picture or illustrate your feelings.

_____
_____
_____
_____
_____
_____
_____
_____

Optional Activities

1. **Listen** — to "Let Them See You," by Colton Dixon. Think about ways you can let others see Christ in your life on a daily basis and in any situation.

2. **Inner Beauty Detective** — Choose one of your close friends or someone you admire or who mentors you. Purchase (or make) a card and write out Galatians 5:22 and Philippians 4:8 in it. Then list 5-10 of the beautiful inner qualities you detect in this person. Mail the card or personally deliver it to her!

3. **Selfless Act** — Do one selfless act of kindness every day this week. Record what you did and any results that were noticeable.

Spending Time Alone with God

Monday: Matthew 6:26-34

Look at the birds of the air; they do not sow or reap or store away in barns, and yet your heavenly Father feeds them. Are you not much more valuable than they? Can any one of you by worrying add a single hour to your life? And why do you worry about clothes? See how the flowers of the field grow. They do not labor or spin. Yet I tell you that not even Solomon in all his splendor was dressed like one of these. If that is how God clothes the grass of the field, which is here today and tomorrow is thrown into the fire, will he not much more clothe you — you of little faith? So do not worry, saying, 'What shall we eat?' or 'What shall we drink?' or 'What shall we wear?' For the pagans run after all these things, and your heavenly Father knows that you need them. But seek first his kingdom and his righteousness, and all these things will be given to you as well. Therefore do not worry about tomorrow, for tomorrow will worry about itself. Each day has enough trouble of its own.

Tuesday: 1 John 1:5-9

This is the message we have heard from him and declare to you: God is light; in him there is no darkness at all. If we claim to have fellowship with him and yet walk in the darkness, we lie and do not live out the truth. But if we walk in the light, as he is in the light, we have fellowship with one another, and the blood of Jesus, his Son, purifies us from all sin. If we claim to be without sin, we deceive ourselves and the truth is not in us. If we confess our sins, he is faithful and just and will forgive us our sins and purify us from all unrighteousness.

Wednesday: Philippians 2:1-4

If you have any encouragement from being united with Christ, if any comfort from his love, if any common sharing in the Spirit, if any tenderness and compassion, then make my joy complete by being like-minded, having the same love, being one in spirit and of one mind. Do nothing out of selfish ambition or vain conceit. Rather, in humility value others above yourselves, not looking to your own interests but each of you to the interests of the others.

Thursday: Ephesians 3:20-21

Now to him who is able to do immeasurably more than all we ask or imagine, according to his power that is at work within us, to him be glory in the church and in Christ Jesus throughout all generations, for ever and ever! Amen.

Friday: Ecclesiastes 3:11

He has made everything beautiful in its time. He has also set eternity in the human heart; yet no one can fathom what God has done from beginning to end.

Chapter 4

No-Regrets Dating

You are not like that, for you are a chosen people. You are royal priests, a holy nation, God's very own possession. As a result, you can show others the goodness of God, for he called you out of the darkness into his wonderful light.

1 Peter 2:9 NLT

Some young women think if they have a special guy then they must be somebody special. Will you settle for any boyfriend just to say that you have one? If your answer is "no," then you must have some idea of the qualifications you are looking for.

What qualities are you looking for in a guy? List them in the spaces provided.

_____ _____ _____

_____ _____ _____

_____ _____ _____

_____ _____ _____

Now, rank them in order of importance.

Is being a Christian on your list? Read 2 Corinthians 6:14. What do you think "unequally yoked" means? How does the word *equal* compare to the phrase *like-minded*?

_____

_____

_____

Can you be a good person and still not be a Christian? Explain.

_____

_____

_____

_____

What kinds of things will you not tolerate?

_____	_____	_____	_____
_____	_____	_____	_____
_____	_____	_____	_____
_____	_____	_____	_____

Why do you think guys want a girlfriend?

_____

_____

_____

Consider what a relationship with a guy involves:

First, cultivating a friendship is time-consuming. Middle school and high school are already busy and potentially stressful times. Even a mature, healthy relationship can be complicated at times. But in middle and high school, a serious or exclusive relationship can lead to more stress. Guys can distract you from focusing on things that should take priority in your life. What are some important things in your life right now?

_____

_____

_____

How can a guy be distracting in any one of these important areas? _____

_____

_____

_____

Second, a relationship should be friendly, simple, and without regrets. This will alleviate the tension that comes with a relationship. What do you think it means to have no regrets? _____

_____

_____

_____

Decide now, before you are emotionally involved with a guy, how far you are willing to go with no regrets. Determine for yourself the physical boundary lines and ask God to help you not cross them.

When a guy really likes you, he will respect you. What does it mean to respect?

_____

_____

_____

He will also respect the people and ideals important in your life. Who are the most important people in your life? _____

_____

_____

_____

In addition, he will respect your beliefs and convictions. And if you are like-minded, he will have the same ones. He will not offend you in his speech or his actions. He should complement you by enhancing your good qualities and encouraging you. Thus, the relationship will please God.

Think about emotional boundaries as well. Emotionally guard your heart against thinking you can change this guy into being more Christ-like, or even what you want him to be. You cannot change a person. And why would you want to? That's God's job. God is working in guys' lives just like He is young women's. He will send the right guy to find you at the perfect time.

Be careful not to make any guy an idol. An idol is anything or anyone who is more important to you than God is. You may think that would never happen. But the way you prioritize your time, and the people you spend it with, speak loudly about what you value most.

Equally important is to not make the judgment that any guy is better than you. If you do that, you could find yourself toying with ideas that since you don't deserve such a great person, you have to compromise your values to keep him.

You are worthy of God's best — always.

Third, a dating relationship must not be sexual. A young woman in her 20s shared this: "Guys who want sex while dating do not respect you. They just want what's easy. A girl they really like will always be respected for her purity."

God is the creator of sex. Besides procreation, sex was designed to be the glue that helps hold a marriage together. Sex within marriage is good. Our culture has made purity and abstinence seem weird or old fashioned. But God knows what is good for us.

Read 1 Corinthians 6:18. What are we to flee? _____

_____

_____

According to Webster's Dictionary, *flee* means to "run away from danger."[4] In other words, get out fast. Write down why you think God says to run fast from sexual impurity.

_____

_____

_____

_____

God knows:

1. You would feel shame and guilt if you engaged in sexual sin — not special, as He intended, but worthless and dirty. He doesn't want you to feel that way. Remember, you are His special treasure and bought with a high price. He sacrificed His own Son for you.

2. Sex can lead to sexually transmitted diseases (STDs). There are approximately 19 million new cases of STDs each year, and 9 million occur among 15-24 year olds.[5] There is a good chance that sex can lead to an unplanned, untimely pregnancy, which may force you to drop out of school. Currently, 750,000 women between the ages of 15-19 become pregnant each year. The good news is that the rate has dropped 41% from its peak in 1990. One of the reasons for the decline is due to the higher proportions of teens choosing to delay sexual activity.[6]

3. An unplanned pregnancy could lead to an abortion. One-third of all teen pregnancies end in abortion. According to studies, the side effects of abortion are guilt, depression, eating disorders, drug and alcohol abuse, and low self-esteem. Low self-esteem, guilt, and depression are contributing factors to suicide.[7]

This is not God's best for you. His desire is to keep you from this kind of pain.

Choosing to be pure may be more popular than you think. One high school junior shared she was having a conversation with a group of girls during class. Before long the subject turned to girls and their promiscuous behaviors. This girl confided that she was pure and intended to save herself for marriage. Many girls chimed in, indicating that they were pure too. Purity became popular that day.

By remaining pure you have nothing to lose but everything to gain. List what you gain.

_____

_____

_____

_____

Can holding your boyfriend's hand eventually lead to sex? Could a kiss lead to sex?

_____

_____

_____

_____

How do you think guys would answer the question if it were reversed? _____

_____

_____

_____

_____

What steps can you take to avoid falling into a sexual situation? _____

_____

_____

_____

If you are already in a relationship, it is very likely that your intentions started out with a desire to please God and remain pure. This is why you need to decide the boundary lines *before* a relationship starts, rather than *after,* when your emotions are way too involved.

Read Ecclesiastes 3:1. What is it telling you?

_____

_____

At *this time* in your life, grades, sports, church, and developing your personal interests are what make the resume for your future. God is at work shaping your character as you pursue His purpose for your life. God is doing the very same thing in the life of your future husband, too. In all of your relationships, the questions you should be asking are as follows:

1. Does this relationship bring out the best in me?
2. Is this relationship helping move me closer to my purpose in life?
3. Does this relationship please God?
4. Is this relationship moving me closer to God?

If the answer to any of these questions is "no," then you shouldn't be in a relationship with that person. Determine to go into a relationship with full confidence of who you are in God's eyes, and come away from it with that same confidence. If you need to end a relationship that isn't God-honoring, you may be sad at the loss of this relationship, but you won't be devastated.

Make the decision to honor God with your body. Decide to remain pure. Asking God to help you keep this commitment will enable you to have no regrets.

Praying for Yourself and Others

Devote yourselves to prayer with an alert mind and a thankful heart.

Colossians 4:2 NLT

What are you praying about this week?

Journaling Your Thoughts

What part of this study meant the most to you? What do you think God is teaching you? Are you having a hard time understanding any part? Ask God to help you believe. Write your thoughts.

Doodling Your Thoughts

Use the space below to draw a picture or illustrate your feelings.

Optional Activities

1. **Bracelet or Anklet** — Look again at the list you made of the qualities you are looking for in a guy. Pick the first 5-6 traits and match them to a color. For example, a Christian = white, funny = red, respectful = blue, etc. Then using scissors, string, and a variety of colored beads from a craft store, string them together to make a bracelet/anklet. Wear it often to remind yourself that you are waiting for the right person.

2. **Purity Ring** — Consider buying a purity ring. There are many different colors and styles to choose from. But you can also purchase any beautiful ring and decide to make it your purity ring.

3. **Letter** — How much time do you spend thinking about the opposite sex? If you notice it's becoming excessive, whisper a prayer to God each time your thoughts begin to focus on a guy. Then, write a letter to your future spouse. Tell him you are praying for him.

Spending Time Alone with God

Monday: Proverbs 3:5-6

Trust in the L<small>ORD</small> with all your heart and lean not on your own understanding; in all your ways submit to him, and he will make your paths straight.

Tuesday: 2 Corinthians 4:7-9, 16-17

We have this treasure in jars of clay to show that this all-surpassing power is from God and not from us. We are hard pressed on every side, but not crushed; perplexed, but not in despair; persecuted, but not abandoned; struck down, but not destroyed....Therefore we do not lose heart. Though outwardly we are wasting away, yet inwardly we are being renewed day by day. For our light and momentary troubles are achieving for us an eternal glory that far outweighs them all.

Wednesday: Philippians 3:12-14

Not that I have already obtained all this, or have already arrived at my goal, but I press on to take hold of that for which Christ Jesus took hold of me. Brothers and sisters, I do not consider myself yet to have taken hold of it. But one thing I do: Forgetting what is behind and straining toward what is ahead, I press on toward the goal to win the prize for which God has called me heavenward in Christ Jesus.

Thursday: Colossians 3:12-17

As God's chosen people, holy and dearly loved, clothe your selves with compassion, kindness, humility, gentleness and patience. Bear with each other and forgive one another if any of you has a grievance against someone. Forgive as the Lord forgave you. And over all these virtues put on love, which binds them all together in perfect unity. Let the peace of Christ rule in your hearts, since as members of one body you were called to peace. And be thankful. Let the message of Christ dwell among you richly as you teach and admonish one another with all wisdom through psalms, hymns, and songs from the Spirit, singing to God with gratitude in your hearts. And whatever you do, whether in word or deed, do it all in the name of the Lord Jesus, giving thanks to God the Father through him.

Friday: Hebrews 4:12, 15-16

The word of God is alive and active. Sharper than any double-edged sword, it penetrates even to dividing soul and spirit, joints and marrow; it judges the thoughts and attitudes of the heart....For we do not have a high priest who is unable to empathize with our weaknesses, but we have one who has been tempted in every way, just as we are — yet he did not sin. Let us then approach God's throne of grace with confidence, so that we may receive mercy and find grace to help us in our time of need.

Chapter 5

Sparkle!

*You were once darkness, but now you are light in the Lord.
Walk as children of light.*

Ephesians 5:8 NKJV

Deciding when to speak and what to say is not only a teen problem. All of humanity has struggled with the gift of gab. Maybe that's why God gives us so much guidance and instruction on this topic. If you haven't found this to be a problem for yourself yet, chances are you will, or that you know someone who has untimely, unfit, discouraging, filthy, gossipy, conversation. The sooner you recognize the repercussions of this type of communication, the sooner you will reap the blessings of self-control.

Maybe you can recall your first deception from this childhood chant: *"Sticks and stones may break my bones, but words can never hurt me."* A little gossip, teasing, or mean word never really hurts anybody, right? When one young teen was asked what was giving her the most trouble in 8th grade, without hesitation she replied, "Gossip, and all the drama that goes with it."

When we shine the light on our careless words we learn the truth and find that words can ignite a fire within us that leaves scars for a lifetime.

Has there been a time someone used words, either spoken or written, that made you feel bad? Maybe it was a lie, or something said in a joking manner, but it hurt deeply. Explain what happened.

_____

_____

_____

_____

Today this kind of verbal abuse is called bullying and it carries serious consequences.

Now think about a time someone said something nice to you. Maybe it was your teacher, or your parents, or a friend. What did they say and how did it make you feel?

_____

_____

_____

_____

Read James 3:5*b*-6. To what does the Scripture compare our tongue?

_____

Often we turn on the television and hear news reports about raging forest fires. These fires were kindled from a single spark. The flames led to complete devastation in the loss of homes, land, and lives. In the same way, a spark from our tongue can kill a relationship, ruin a reputation, become wrapped up in filthy gossip, and destroy a Christian's witness.

Now read James 3:3-4. Our tongues are compared to two objects. What are these objects and what are they used for?

1. _____
   _____

2. _____
   _____

Each is so small yet possesses great power. A small bit controls a strong and powerful animal and the rudder directs a boat. Our tongues are small too, but like the bit and rudder they hold great power. Proverbs 12:18 tells us words can pierce a person's heart like a sword. This may be a morbid thought but we must consider it. What can a sword through the heart do?

_____

Now think about how your words can bring an emotional death. You may go to church regularly, pray every morning at breakfast, sing in the youth choir, and go on mission trips. But the Bible says if anyone among you thinks he is religious, and does not bridle his tongue, but deceives his own heart, this one's religion is useless. (James 1:26 NKJV) This is a strong admonishment that must be taken seriously. What does Psalm 39:1 suggest you can put on your mouth to help you live righteously? _____

Ephesians 4:29 directs us to not use any foul or abusive language. You probably hear foul language throughout the day in your school or work environment, at the movies, or on television. Anyone can use filthy language, curse words, and God's name irreverently. It takes a person with self-control and confidence to go against the norm.

How can having a foul mouth take away from your femininity? _____

_____

_____

_____

Proverbs 16:28 (NKJV) refers to a gossip as a whisperer. What will happen to a friendship if the gossip continues? _____

_____

Match the following references to the verse.

    1 Timothy 5:13   Talking a lot brings a greater chance to sin.

    Proverbs 15:28   A gossip reveals secrets.

    Proverbs 20:19   Righteous people know how to answer.

    Proverbs 11:13   Avoid people who gossip/talk too much.

    Proverbs 10:19   Gossipers are also called busybodies.

Do you know which girls in your class or club are gossips?   Yes   No

What do you want to be known as — a person who spreads rumors and says mean and hateful things, or someone who is kind and considerate and keeps confidences?

Do you need to initiate any changes to restore your reputation? If so, what?

_____

_____

_____

What will you continue to do to keep yourself in good standing with your peers?

_____

_____

_____

A word of caution: Loving your friend means you care about what happens to her. If ever your friend tells you a secret that could put her life or another person's life in danger, tell an adult you trust. This will protect your friend. When are times you should tell a trusted adult a secret?

_____

_____

_____

Think back on a time you made a big bowl of popcorn and salted it. What did the salt do to the popcorn? _____

Salt does more than add flavor. It is a preservative and also acts as a healing agent. Read Colossians 4:6. What does our speech need to be seasoned with?

_____

_____

As Christian young women, we bring flavor into others' lives when we bring uplifting, gentle, thoughtful, and encouraging words. Then we will make their hearts glad. Read the following verses and write the result of using good words in a thoughtful way.

Proverbs 15:1 _____

_____

Proverbs 15:4 _____

_____

Proverbs 16:24 _____

_____

In Matthew 12:34-35 we learn that our speech is evidence of our inward character and a reflection of our hearts. A young woman who is shining the light will use her words to point others to her faith in Jesus.

Because we are human, we will make mistakes and sometimes fail to think before we speak or become involved in gossip.

Confess your mistake to God and then start over. Ask God to help you in this area of self-control. This is all part of becoming a young woman of God.

Praying for Yourself and Others

Are any of you suffering hardships? You should pray.
Are any of you happy? You should sing praises.

James 5:13 NLT

What are you praying about this week?

_____

_____

_____

_____

_____

_____

_____

_____

_____

_____

_____

_____

_____

_____

_____

Journaling Your Thoughts

What part of this study meant the most to you? What do you think God is teaching you? Are you having a hard time understanding any part? Ask God to help you believe. Write your thoughts.

_____

_____

_____

_____

_____

_____

_____

_____

_____

_____

_____

_____

_____

_____

_____

_____

Doodling Your Thoughts and Feelings

Use this page to draw a picture or illustrate your feelings.

Optional Activities

1. **Gossip Calendar** — Studies suggest that it takes 21 days to develop a new habit. Try not to gossip for 21 days. Use a calendar to record your progress. For each day you are successful, write, "Thank you, God!" on the date. If you slip into your old pattern, confess your sin to God, forgive yourself, and write on the calendar date, "Help me start again."

2. **Encouragement Notes** — Make a list of your friends and family members who could use some encouragement. Over the next month make it your goal to send one note each week. Think about creative places to leave the encouraging note. For example, on a mirror, on a car dashboard, in a backpack, or in a book.

Spending Time Alone with God

Monday: Proverbs 26:20-28

Without wood a fire goes out; without a gossip a quarrel dies down. As charcoal to embers and as wood to fire, so is a quarrelsome person for kindling strife. The words of a gossip are like choice morsels; they go down to the inmost parts. Like a coating of silver dross on earthenware are fervent lips with an evil heart. Enemies disguise themselves with their lips, but in their hearts they harbor deceit. Though their speech is charming, do not believe them, for seven abominations fill their hearts. Their malice may be concealed by deception, but their wickedness will be exposed in the assembly. Whoever digs a pit will fall into it; if someone rolls a stone, it will roll back on them. A lying tongue hates those it hurts, and a flattering mouth works ruin.

Tuesday: Proverbs 12:25

Anxiety weighs down the heart, but a kind word cheers it up.

Wednesday: Proverbs 16:23-28

The hearts of the wise make their mouths prudent, and their lips promote instruction. Gracious words are a honeycomb, sweet to the soul and healing to the bones. There is a way that appears to be right, but in the end it leads to death. The appetite of laborers works for them; their hunger drives them on. A scoundrel plots evil, and on their lips it is like a scorching fire. A perverse person stirs up conflict, and a gossip separates close friends.

Thursday: Philippians 4:13

I can do all this through him who gives me strength.

Friday: Lamentations 3:22-26

Because of the LORD's great love we are not consumed, for his compassions never fail. They are new every morning; great is your faithfulness. I say to myself, "The LORD is my portion; therefore I will wait for him." The LORD is good to those whose hope is in him, to the one who seeks him; it is good to wait quietly for the salvation of the LORD.

Chapter 6

Fabulous Friendship

O send out Your light and truth! Let them lead me.

Psalm 43:3 NKJV

Studies done on friendships conclude that the average person has a core group of close, special friends…those you spend time with and share your dreams. These core friends, can be counted on one hand. *Just one hand!*

Who are your best (core) friends, including girls outside this group? Write their names.

_____

_____

_____

_____

_____

Read the following verse on friendship and summarize what it says.

Proverbs 27:17 _____

_____

When you rub two iron blades together the edges become sharper. How do you think you can sharpen your friend? _____

_____

_____

_____

Proverbs 17:17 _____

_____

What does it mean that a friend is born for adversity? _____

_____

_____

Romans 12:15 _____

_____

Why do you think Christians do this? _____

_____

_____

1 Corinthians 15:33 _____

_____

The Bible gives us examples of friendships.

As soon as he had finished speaking to Saul, the soul of Jonathan was knit to the soul of David, and Jonathan loved him as his own soul. And Saul took him that day and would not let him return to his father's house. Then Jonathan made a covenant with David, because he loved him as his own soul. (1 Samuel 18:1-3 ESV)

And: *Ruth said, "Do not urge me to leave you or to turn back from following you; For where you go, I will go, and where you lodge, I will lodge. Your people shall be my people, and your God, my God. Where you die, I will die, and there I will be buried. Thus may the LORD do to me, and worse, if anything but death parts you and me.* (Ruth 1:16-17 NASB)

Read John 11:35. Jesus was at the tomb of His friend Lazarus immediately before He raised Lazarus from the dead. What does John say Jesus did? _____

Read John 11:36. How did the onlookers react? What did they say?

_____

_____

The love between friends is very special. There are healthy guidelines for choosing or accepting a core friend. Core friends share these five traits:

1. **Love of God.** Your closest friends should love God and share your morals and values. This is very important because when you need prayer, encouragement, or advice, you can know that your friend is also seeking God's will for you. It is also important that a friend hold you accountable to those Christian values and truths. She won't just "agree" with you out of fear that she will hurt your feelings. She will say, "Let's pray about this" and "Let's look to God's Word to see what He would have you do."

2. **Respect.** Even if you have a difference of opinion, not related to your spiritual beliefs, you should respect each other. You and your friend are uniquely made! Closest friends share similar beliefs, morals, and values, but you may be very different in style! For example, you differ in athleticism, fashion, how you spend your time, and how you use your gifts, to name a few things.

3. **Love.** You can only love another if you first feel worthy of love yourself. To Jesus, you were worth dying on the cross so He could have a relationship with you. He loves you! To show love to your friend you can:
    - Provide help when she needs it.
    - Pray with and for her.
    - Be her best cheerleader!
    - Speak well of her.
    - Give material gifts…homemade or store-bought.

4. **Humility.** Friendship isn't a competition. Be willing to take second place and let your friend shine. Friendships have ended because of pride and jealousy. You may have a sweet, perfect friendship, but keep in mind people are not perfect. When you make a mistake say you're sorry.

5. **Loyalty.** Relationships are "give and take." There may be seasons when one is less able to "give" because of her circumstances, but there needs to be a balance in the long run. One person can't always be giving and the other person always receiving.

As you continue to grow and develop into the unique individual God created you to be, your likes and dislikes may change. Friendships can change because people change. The ending of a friendship isn't always hurtful. Sometimes it's more like a quiet disconnect. But other times when a friendship doesn't work out, it can feel like betrayal and leave you feeling sad.

Jesus experienced betrayal. Anytime you are worried about a friendship or experience betrayal you can talk to Jesus about it. He knows exactly how you feel.

Surround yourself with friends who will help you grow in your relationship with the Lord, encourage you, and pray for you. This will lighten your burdens and make the dark times not seem so dark.

Praying for Yourself and Others

The earnest prayer of a righteous person has great power and produces wonderful results.

James 5:16 NLT

What are you praying about this week?

Journaling and Doodling Your Thoughts and Feelings

What part of this study meant the most to you? What do you think God is teaching you? Are you having a hard time understanding any part? Ask God to help you believe. Write your thoughts. You can also use the space below the lines to draw a picture or illustrate your feelings.

_____

_____

_____

_____

_____

_____

_____

_____

Optional Activities

1. **Daily Reminder Clock** — Decide a time of day when you can pray specifically for a friend. Then, using an index card, draw a picture of a clock and set the hands to the time you commit to pray for her. Post this clock where you are reminded to pray.

2. **Bake Something Yummy** — Make muffins, cookies or a cake as a "just because" gift for your friend. Wrap them in pretty paper or a decorated bag. Put a bow on top!

3. **Make Her a Card** — Include in it "25 Great Things About You."

Spending Time Alone with God

Monday: 1 Corinthians 13:4-7

Love is patient, love is kind. It does not envy, it does not boast, it is not proud. It does not dishonor others, it is not self-seeking, it is not easily angered, it keeps no record of wrongs. Love does not delight in evil but rejoices with the truth. It always protects, always trusts, always hopes, always perseveres.

Tuesday: Philippians 4:6-7

Do not be anxious about anything, but in every situation, by prayer and petition, with thanksgiving, present your requests to God. And the peace of God, which transcends all understanding, will guard your hearts and your minds in Christ Jesus.

Wednesday: Zephaniah 3:17

The Lord your God is with you, the Mighty Warrior who saves. He will take great delight in you; in his love he will no longer rebuke you, but will rejoice over you with singing.

Thursday: Psalm 1

Blessed is the one who does not walk in step with the wicked or stand in the way that sinners take or sit in the company of mockers, but whose delight is in the law of the Lord, and who meditates on his law day and night. That person is like a tree planted by streams of water, which yields its fruit in season and whose leaf does not wither — whatever they do prospers. Not so the wicked! They are like chaff that the wind blows away. Therefore the wicked will not stand in the judgment, nor sinners in the assembly of the righteous. For the Lord watches over the way of the righteous, but the way of the wicked leads to destruction.

Friday: Joshua 1:7-9

Be strong and very courageous. Be careful to obey all the law my servant Moses gave you; do not turn from it to the right or to the left, that you may be successful wherever you go. Keep this Book of the Law always on your lips; meditate on it day and night, so that you may be careful to do everything written in it. Then you will be prosperous and successful. Have I not commanded you? Be strong and courageous. Do not be afraid; do not be discouraged, for the Lord your God will be with you wherever you go.

Chapter 7

Rising Above the Darkness

*You are my lamp, O L*ORD*; The L*ORD *shall enlighten my darkness.*

2 Samuel 22:29 NKJV

The barrage of decisions you face daily can feel like heavy storm clouds hanging over you, eclipsing your light. This is not exclusively a teen issue. All women have days when stress has caused them to be emotionally and physically tired. Learning how to minimize the daily pressures while you're young will help you handle problems — large and small — and keep you from unnecessary pain.

Look at the following list of synonyms for stressed. Circle any that apply to you.

overwhelmed	worried	busy
exhausted	torn	confused
dazed	overcome	distracted
hectic	anxious	other_____

Describe how social media makes you feel. For example: Do posts on Snapchat, Instagram, or Facebook ever make you jealous? List 5-10 adjectives that describe the possible emotions you feel or could feel. _____

_____

_____

If you're not on social media, who or what influences how you feel? _____

_____

_____

How would you describe your day? _____

_____

_____

_____

What makes you most exhausted? _____

_____

_____

_____

What activities in your life do you consider good or worthwhile? _____

_____

_____

Taking on too many activities, even good activities, can lead to stress. How does being too busy affect your body?

Physically_____

_____

_____

Emotionally_____

_____

_____

Mentally _____

_____

_____

Spiritually _____

_____

_____

Read 1 Peter 5:6-8. How is Satan described? _____

Recall John 10:10. Satan (the thief) comes only to _____ and

_____ and _____.

Satan wants to tear you apart like a fierce lion would his prey. If he can keep you too busy, distracted from the important things, and away from time with God, then you won't grow in your relationship with Christ, and you won't bring others to Him, either. He also knows that busyness leads to frustration, chaos, and disappointment.

Describe a time when Satan used busyness to distract you. _____

_____

_____

Do you sometimes feel confused about plans or decisions? Confusion is Satan's weapon. This is not God's plan for you. Paul told the Corinthians, *"God is not the author of confusion but of peace."* (1 Corinthians 14:33 NKJV) God does not bring confusion. Furthermore, Paul told Timothy, *"God has not given us a spirit of fearfulness, but one of power, love, and sound judgment."* (2 Timothy 1:7 HCSB) Sound judgment is your ability to assess situations and then draw sound conclusions.

Read Jeremiah 17:8. God tells us to stretch out our roots by the river and drink when the heat comes. What is causing you the most heat right now? What are you most worried about? _____

_____

Are any of these on your list? Circle all that apply.

pleasing parents	making the team	pressure from friends
college applications	perfectionist tendencies	lack of money
good grades	friends	disruptive home life
weight	a boyfriend	someone to sit with at lunch

These are not silly problems. Jesus has the only solution. He said, *"Come to me, all who are weary and burdened, and I will give you rest.* (Matthew 11:28) Jesus desires to help you make sense of your problems and then deal with them appropriately.

Read 2 Corinthians 4:8-9 and fill in the missing words.

We are hard pressed on every side, yet not _____; We are perplexed, but not in _____; Persecuted, but not _____; Struck down, but not _____.

Now read James 1:2-4. What do you think this means? _____
_____
_____

First Peter 1:6-7 tells us: *Be truly glad. There is wonderful joy ahead, even though you have to endure many trials for a little while. These trials will show that your faith is genuine. It is being tested as fire tests and purifies gold — though your faith is far more precious than mere gold. So when your faith remains strong through many trials, it will bring you much praise and glory and honor on the day when Jesus Christ is revealed to the whole world.* (NLT)

Circle the word in that passage that tells what fire purifies.

When you feel the "heat" of the fire during hard times, it means you are being purified just as gold becomes purified when placed in the fire. You become stronger in your faith and closer to God. Increasing your faith and becoming closer to God is where the joy comes from. In that same passage, underline the phrase *you may have to endure trials for a little while*. It can feel like the trials in your life are never-ending, but take heart because they will end. God knows what's around the corner! You can trust Him. You are His most important priority!

Problems. Stress. Trials. People going through hard times call it different things. The Bible often refers to them as storms. Read Matthew 7:24-25. When this physical storm came about, why didn't the house fall? _____

When your storms come, your rock is Jesus. He is your strong and steady foundation that will keep you from being tossed.

Read Philippians 4:13. What are *all things*? Make this personal. Fill in the blank with two or three of your most pressing problems.

I can _____
because God gives me strength.

I can _____
because God gives me strength.

I can _____
because God gives me strength.

Look again at your list of worries/stresses. Proverbs 12:15 tells us *the way of fools seems right to them, but the wise listen to advice*. It helps to talk over your problems, especially when it involves making a decision. Who do you consider to be a godly friend or mentor? List a name or two on the line below, and communicate with them often.

_____

_____

Read Luke 1:37 and Jeremiah 32:17b. What can't God do? What is too hard for Him?

___

___

That's right! Say that ten times or as many times as necessary until you believe it.

Below you will find several scripture passages. Read them often to receive peace, joy, rest, and direction. Do more than read — believe.

Psalm 50:15	Call on Me in the day of trouble and I will deliver you, and you will honor Me.
1 Peter 5:7	Cast all your anxiety on him because he cares for you.
Psalm 27:1 (NLT)	The LORD is my light and my salvation — so why should I be afraid? The LORD is my fortress, protecting me from danger, so why should I tremble?
Psalm 25:4-5 (NASB)	Make me know Your ways, O LORD; Teach me Your paths. Lead me in Your truth and teach me, For You are the God of my salvation; For You I wait all the day.
Psalm 91:4	He will cover you with His feathers, and under His wings you will find refuge; His faithfulness will be your shield and rampart.
Psalm 32:8	I will instruct you and teach you in the way you should go; I will counsel you with my loving eye on you.
John 14:13-14	I will do whatever you ask in my name, so that the Father may be glorified in the Son. You may ask me for anything in my name, and I will do it.
Psalm 119:18 (NLT)	Open my eyes to see the wonderful truths in your instructions.
Philippians 4:6 (NLT)	Don't worry about anything; instead, pray about everything. Tell God what you need, and thank him for all he has done.

Psalm 18:6 (NASB)	*In my distress I called upon the L*ORD*, And cried to my God for help; He heard my voice out of His temple, And my cry for help before Him came into His ears.*
Isaiah 30:21 (NASB)	*Your ears will hear a word behind you, "This is the way, walk in it," whenever you turn to the right or to the left.*
Jeremiah 33:3 (NASB)	*Call to Me and I will answer you, and I will tell you great and mighty things, which you do not know.*
Isaiah 41:10 (HCSB)	*Do not fear, I am with you; do not be afraid, for I am your God. I will strengthen you; I will help you; I will hold on to you with My righteous right hand.*

Jesus said we need something. Read Mark 6:31 and record what we need.

_____

_____

Be intentional about planning time to rest. When is a good time for you to rest? What do you like to do that is restful? _____

_____

_____

_____

_____

A joyless, hopeless, disposition negatively changes your countenance (appearance). But when you lay your problems and fears before a Mighty God, and then trust Him to lead and guide you, your joy will be restored and a smile will return to your face.

Praying for Yourself and Others

*We are confident that he hears us whenever we ask
for anything that pleases him.*

1 John 5:14 NLT

What are you praying about this week?

_____

_____

_____

_____

_____

_____

_____

_____

_____

_____

_____

_____

_____

_____

_____

Journaling Your Thoughts

What part of this study meant the most to you? What do you think God is teaching you? Are you having a hard time understanding any part? Ask God to help you believe. Write your thoughts.

_____

_____

_____

_____

_____

_____

_____

_____

_____

_____

_____

_____

_____

_____

_____

_____

_____

_____

_____

Doodling Your Thoughts and Feelings

Use this page to draw a picture or illustrate your feelings.

Optional Activities

1. **Personal Time-out** — Plan a few hours of alone time for just you and God. Grab your Bible, a journal, or maybe a devotional book, and a pen or pencil. Pack a snack and head to the park, the front porch, the hammock in the yard, or any place that is quiet, safe, and peaceful to have some time alone to hear God's gentle whisper.

2. **Counteract the Negative** — Balance negative thoughts and criticisms with praise and thanksgiving for one day. Keep a note pad with you from the time you get up until you go to bed. For every complaint, criticism, and negative thought about yourself or another person, write down one thing you are thankful for. Most of us do not give God the praise He is worthy of, so this can be the start to a good habit. A thankful heart is like medicine for the soul.

3. **Soothing Face Mask** — Make a mask using ¼ cup raw honey, 2 tablespoons nutmeg, and 1 tablespoon cinnamon. Mix the ingredients to form a paste. Apply it to your clean face and neck, avoiding the eye area. Leave the mask on about 25 minutes, then rinse it off with warm water. You can find more mask recipes at: www.acneskinsite.com/homemade-facials/

Spending Time Alone with God

Monday: Exodus 20:7

You shall not misuse the name of the Lord your God, for the Lord will not hold anyone guiltless who misuses his name.

Tuesday: Psalm 118:24

The Lord has done it this very day; let us rejoice today and be glad

Wednesday: Psalm 51:10

Create in me a pure heart, O God, and renew a steadfast spirit within me.

Thursday: Nehemiah 1:4-6

When I heard these things, I sat down and wept. For some days I mourned and fasted and prayed before the God of heaven. Then I said: "Lord, the God of heaven, the great and awesome God, who keeps his covenant of love with those who love him and keep his commandments, let your ear be attentive and your eyes open to hear the prayer your servant is praying before you day and night for your servants, the people of Israel. I confess the sins we Israelites, including myself and my father's family, have committed against you."

Friday: Isaiah 55:6-11

Seek the Lord while he may be found; call on him while he is near. Let the wicked forsake their ways and the unrighteous their thoughts. Let them turn to the Lord, and he will have mercy on them, and to our God, for he will freely pardon. "For my thoughts are not your thoughts, neither are your ways my ways," declares the Lord. As the heavens are higher than the earth, so are my ways higher than your ways and my thoughts than your thoughts. As the rain and the snow come down from heaven, and do not return to it without watering the earth and making it bud and flourish, so that it yields seed for the sower and bread for the eater, so is my word that goes out from my mouth: It will not return to me empty, but will accomplish what I desire and achieve the purpose for which I sent it.

Chapter 8

You've Got Talent

*The Light shines in the darkness,
and the darkness can never extinguish it.*

John 1:5 NLT

When God designed you, He embedded within you particular passions, abilities, and talents. These attributes enable you to fulfill your purpose, advance God's kingdom, bring glory and attention to God, and serve others. He intended for you to make a difference.

Read Psalm 20:4 and fill in the blanks. *May God give you the* _____ *of your heart and fulfill all your* _____ .

What do you desire right now? In other words, what are you passionate about? What do you do well? What are your interests? For example, do you like working with children in your church, participating in sports, playing music, reading? _____

_____

_____

_____

Your school, church, and community offer an array of activities and events. List any in which you participate. _____

_____

_____

_____

Your current activities, interests, and talents can indicate how you will spend your time in the future.

God knows your future — five years from now and beyond. And the best news is, He is equipping and preparing you. The author shares her personal story:

> When I was in the 7th grade, my pastor invited me to take the sign language class that was being offered at our church. It was free and I had nothing better to do, so I took the class. I surprised myself when I discovered I was very good at learning to sign. Within just a short period of time I was good enough to sign for the deaf who attended the church services.
>
> I enjoyed signing and had fun with it, but I had no idea what God was really up to in my life.
>
> Five years later, when I was a senior in high school I thought I could not afford to go to college. I applied anyway. Imagine my surprise when I was accepted into a university that needed an interpreter for deaf students. I was hired as their interpreter and was compensated for my work. For four years that job paid for most of my tuition.
>
> You see, the talent God gave me in 7th grade was my ticket to college. I wasn't even thinking about college or my future then, but God sure was![8]

God is working in your life in the same way…right now.

Joseph recognized that his ability to discern and interpret dreams was a gift from God. Let's do a quick review of the highlights of this Bible story. Joseph (age 17) was a shepherd who had prophetic dreams — dreams in which he could see the future. He dreamt he ruled over his brothers.

Read Genesis 37:5. To whom did he tell this dream? _____

His brothers hated his words and his dreams. They were already jealous of Joseph's relationship with their father, and the coat their father had given him, so this new dream just fanned the flames. Genesis 37:28 tells us Joseph's jealous brothers sold him as a slave to get rid of him. Many years passed and Joseph suffered countless trials. Jump ahead to Genesis 41. Pharaoh was having troubling dreams. Read verses 14-15. What did the Pharaoh want Joseph to do?

Joseph used his gift of interpretation, and because he was able to interpret Pharaoh's dreams, Pharaoh made Joseph ruler over Egypt.

In Hebrews 13:20-21 we read this: *Now the God of peace, who brought up from the dead the great Shepherd of the sheep through the blood of the eternal covenant, even Jesus our Lord, equip you in every good thing to do His will, working in us that which is pleasing in His sight, through Jesus Christ, to whom be the glory forever and ever. Amen.* (NASB)

Circle the word *equip*. What do you think this word means? _____

_____

The Macmillan Dictionary defines *equip* this way: "To provide a person, object, or place, with the thing that they need for a particular purpose."9 God has equipped you with gifts and abilities.

First Corinthians 12:7 says *a spiritual gift is given to each of us so we can help each other.* (NLT)

Read and summarize 1 Peter 4:10. _____

_____

_____

Does everyone get the same gift?   YES   NO

Does God expect you to use your gift?   YES   NO

God has equipped you with the tools to share your gift. Tools can be your personal attributes, your passions, and even the people He places in your life. What tools do you think He has given you? _____

_____

_____

Right now you may be involved in several activities you are working to perfect. You probably have to invest time in practice, performance, and meetings. How much time do you allot for these activities? _____

_____

_____

_____

Do you have a lot of activities? Developing your gifts takes time and energy. You may need to let go of some things that are less interesting to you.

Which three activities are of the highest priority? _____

_____

_____

During your quiet moments with God, ask Him to help you identify your gifts and talents. Ask Him to give you the burning desire to pursue those gifts and talents that will lead you straight into the will of God and bring Him glory.

Ask God to help you perfect your gifts. Then, using your gifts to serve Him, you will naturally glow in any situation.

Praying for Yourself and Others

Rejoice in our confident hope.
Be patient in trouble, and keep on praying.

Romans 12:12 NLT

What are you praying about this week?

Journaling Your Thoughts

What part of this study meant the most to you? What do you think God is teaching you? Are you having a hard time understanding any part? Ask God to help you believe. Write your thoughts.

_____

_____

_____

_____

_____

_____

_____

_____

_____

_____

_____

_____

_____

_____

_____

Doodling Your Thoughts and Feelings

Use this page to draw a picture or illustrate your feelings.

Optional Activities

1. **Bubble Organizer** — You may not know where you will be five years from now, but brainstorming where you would like to be can help you take steps in accomplishing your goals. Think about the questions in this chapter: *What are you passionate about? How has God equipped you? What are your gifts?* Using the bubble map on the next page, in the center circle write what you hope to be doing after high school. Then in each circle surrounding it, record a way that will help you achieve that goal. For example, if you record in the center circle that you desire to finish college, then write in a smaller circle, "stay in high school and make good grades." Refer to this bubble map often to encourage you to stay focused on your goals.

2. **Talent Show** — Participate in a talent show showcasing your unique skills and talents.

Bubble Organizer

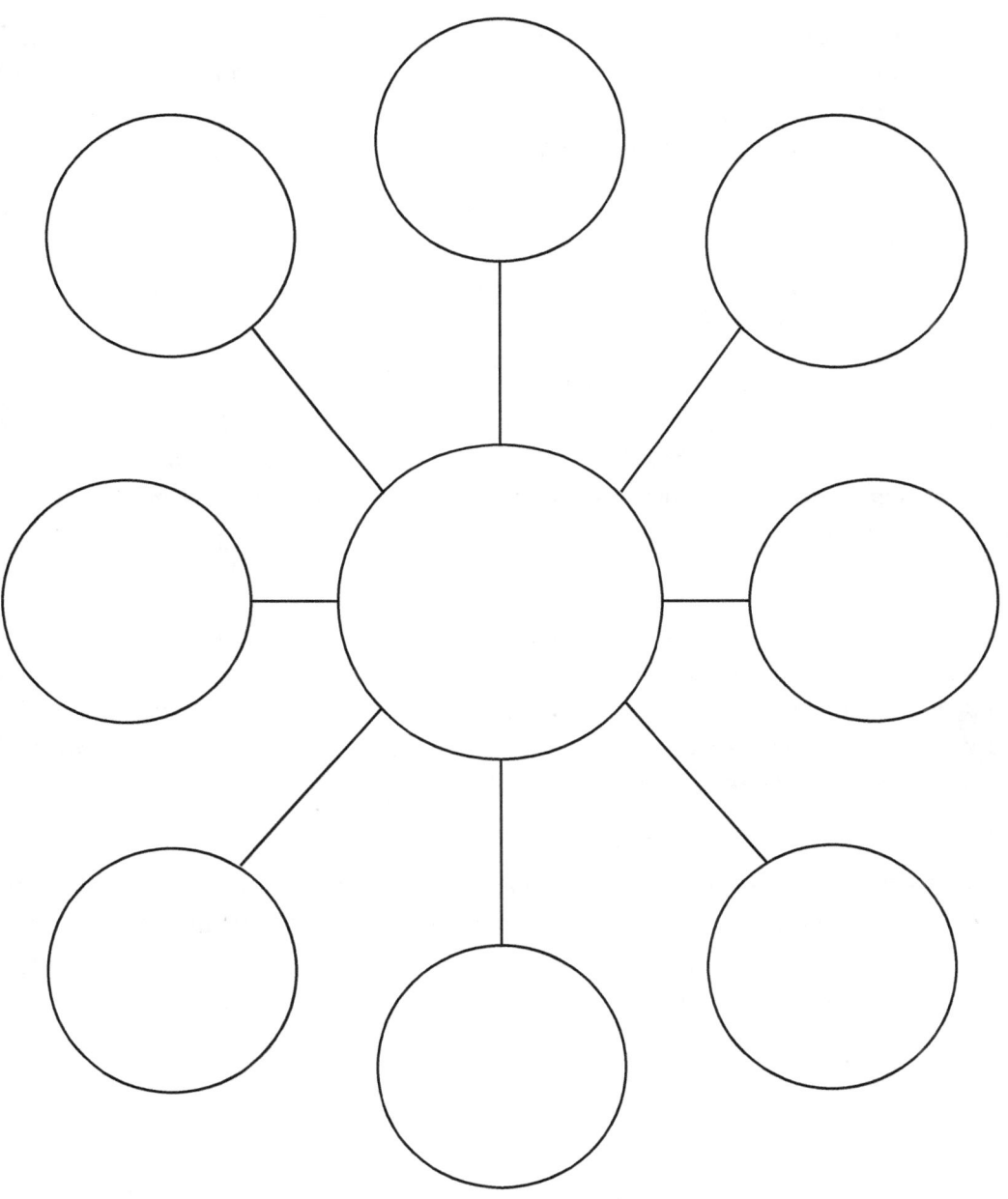

Spending Time Alone with God

Monday: Psalm 66:1-5

Shout for joy to God, all the earth! Sing the glory of his name; make his praise glorious. Say to God, "How awesome are your deeds!" So great is your power that your enemies cringe before you. All the earth bows down to you; they sing praise to you, they sing the praises of your name." Come and see what God has done, his awesome deeds for mankind!

Tuesday: 1 Samuel 16:7

The Lord said to Samuel, "Do not consider his appearance or his height, for I have rejected him. The Lord does not look at the things people look at. People look at the outward appearance, but the Lord looks at the heart."

Wednesday: Psalm 40:1-3

I waited patiently for the Lord; he turned to me and heard my cry. He lifted me out of the slimy pit, out of the mud and mire; he set my feet on a rock and gave me a firm place to stand. He put a new song in my mouth, a hymn of praise to our God. Many will see and fear the Lord and put their trust in him.

Thursday: Psalm 86

Hear me, Lord, and answer me, for I am poor and needy. Guard my life, for I am faithful to you; save your servant who trusts in you. You are my God; have mercy on me, Lord, for I call to you all day long. Bring joy to your servant, Lord, for I put my trust in you. You, Lord, are forgiving and good, abounding in love to all who call to you. Hear my prayer, Lord; listen to my cry for mercy. When I am in distress, I call to you, because you answer me.

Friday: Psalm 86:10-13

You are great and do marvelous deeds; you alone are God. Teach me your way, Lord, that I may rely on your faithfulness; give me an undivided heart, that I may fear your name. I will praise you, Lord my God, with all my heart; I will glorify your name forever. For great is your love toward me; you have delivered me from the depths, from the realm of the dead.

Chapter 9

Glitter

You will light my lamp; the Lord my God will enlighten my darkness.

Psalm 18:28 NKJV

*I*f living as a Christian young woman appears too hard for you, you are right. Everything about living contrary to the world's ideas *is* too hard…when you attempt it on your own. Do you know what *glitter* means? It means to shine with a bright, shimmering, *reflected* light. The moon on its own is dark 24/7, but when the moon reflects the sun, it shines brightly because it reflects something bright. For you to shine brightly, you need to reflect the Son. Jesus will help you live righteously. Releasing this burden to God also takes away a mound of stress!

You can count on this promise: Time alone with God will change your life forever, if you meet with Him daily.

Read Psalm 1:2-3 and fill in the missing words.

His delight is in the _____of the Lord, and on His law he _____ day and night. He is like a _____ planted by streams of_____which yields its_____ in season and whose leaf does not wither. Whatever he does prospers.

You are like this tree. When you spend time with God reading Scripture, you receive nourishment that causes you to mature in Christ and produce the Fruit of the Spirit. (See Galatians 5:22.) Instead of withering up and drying out in the difficult season, you will be restored, renewed, and refreshed! But if you choose to neglect your spiritual life, you won't produce the fruit of the spirit, and God's shining light will grow dim.

Hebrews 2:1 says to "heed" the things we've learned or we will drift away. What does it

mean to heed? _____
_____

When you're not reading God's Word and spending time in prayer, you *will* begin to drift away. It is imperative that you be intentional about making time in your busy days for God. We can always make time for what we value.

Read and summarize James 4:8. _____
_____
_____

To draw near to God, put these things into practice:

1. Find a quiet spot free from distractions. This means away from your phone, your computer, and anything else that would cause your thoughts to start wandering. Your spot might be in your room or a special place in your house. Some things to have on hand include a journal to record your thoughts, your Bible, a devotional guide, praise music, pens and highlighters.

    What other things do you think could be useful? _____
    _____
    _____

    Where is your special place? _____
    _____

    When is the best time of day for you? _____
    _____

    Begin by simply saying *thank you*. Write the date on the top line of your journal page. Then write the word, *Thanksgiving*. List a few things you are thankful for. For example:
    - Cute new shoes to match my skirt
    - Friends to study with

- That I'm not sick anymore
- My Bible
- That you, God, are with me during this very hard time

Psalm 50:14 and 50:23 say that offering praise and thanksgiving to God brings Him glory. When you come to God with a thankful heart, it's like you are opening the conversation with Him, which moves you into the presence of God. And it pleases God when you thank Him. Circumstances aren't always good and you may not feel like saying thanks. Doing so, however, is an act of obedience. It's easy to say thank you to God for the vocal solo you earn in the choir presentation, but what about when your best friend moves away? In times like these, you can admit you're broken-hearted and then thank God that He will be with you during the hard times.

2. Read your Bible and/or devotional guide. The Bible is God's love letter to you. His inspired words are like a map or compass. Read 2 Timothy 3:16-17. What three things is Scripture profitable for? _____, _____, and _____.

3. God's Word is also a source of inspiration, strength and encouragement. Think about a time when you needed to be encouraged and you found something special for yourself in God's word. What was it? If you haven't experienced this yet, wait to answer this until you do.

_____

_____

Pastor Charles Stanley once said, "Making Scripture your daily companion is the best way not to miss God's plan. Without significant time in the Word, we tend to forget what matters to God. When we start mixing the world's lies with the Father's truth, we step out of His plan."[10]

There are many versions of the Bible. Choose one that is easy for you to understand. Devotionals are also good guides, especially when you don't know where to start reading in the Bible. (See Recommended Devotional Guides.)

4. In your journal, record the passages you read. You can summarize what you read, or you can write out exactly the verses you read. This will help you memorize Scripture, too.

5. Apply what you read to your life. The scriptures are not just historical events written for other people. They are written for you. As an example, make them personal by inserting your name, into the following verses:

   Call to Me, _____and I will answer you, and show you great and mighty things, which you do not know. Jeremiah 33:3

   Cast your cares on Him, _____, for He cares for you. 1 Peter 5:7

   To apply the second verse, in your journal make a list of everything you're worried about. Read the list to God during your prayer time.

6. Pray. God desires a relationship with you. Communication is a key component to building relationship. When we communicate with God we develop a deeper relationship with Him. Your relationship with God is very personal — none other knows you and loves you like God does. Therefore there isn't a formality to prayer. It's personal.

   But consider these things when praying:

   - Understand to whom you are praying. He is God! Matthew 8:23-27 tells how Jesus instantly stilled the wind and the waves. He is powerful and Creator of the Universe and all life. Pray like you believe this. Pray honest and big. Tell Him everything. His mercy, grace, love, and forgiveness are limitless.

   - Realize that prayer is communicating at your comfort level. It is not necessary to pray fancy prayers or to use big words. Just pray what is on your heart using your own vocabulary. When you are not sure what to say you can simply say, "Help me."

   - Communication involves both listening and speaking. Take time to be quiet and allow God to speak to your Spirit.

Ask Him to

- forgive your sins. Sin stands in the way of communication with God. Psalm 66:18 tells us if we regard iniquity in our heart, the Lord will not hear. You can pray Psalm 51:10: *Create in me a clean heart, O God, and renew a steadfast spirit within me.* (NKJV)
- help you understand the message you read in your Bible. (James 1:5)
- open your eyes to see what He wants you to see. (Psalm 119:18)

Spending time alone with God changes everything. He alone knows the future and can guide you into his good and perfect plan. You will still have troubles in this world, but God will get you through them.

Match His promises:

1 John 4:4 (NASB)	*These things I have spoken to you, so that in Me you may have peace. In the world you have tribulation, but take courage; I have overcome the world.*
John 16:33 (NASB)	*You, dear children, are from God and have overcome them, because the one who is in you is greater than the one who is in the world.*

With God in your life you will be able to radiate the victory you have in being His child wherever you go.

Praying for Yourself and Others

Answer me when I call to you,

O God who declares me innocent.

Free me from my troubles.

Have mercy on me and hear my prayer.

Psalm 4:1

What are you praying about this week?

_____

_____

_____

_____

_____

_____

_____

_____

_____

_____

_____

_____

_____

_____

Journaling Your Thoughts

What part of this study meant the most to you? What do you think God is teaching you? Are you having a hard time understanding any part? Ask God to help you believe. Write your thoughts.

_____

_____

_____

_____

_____

_____

_____

_____

_____

_____

_____

_____

_____

_____

_____

Doodling Your Thoughts and Feelings

Use this page to draw a picture or illustrate your feelings.

Optional Activities

1. **Journal** — Buy a plain journal at a general merchandise store. Using stickers and markers, personalize your journal.

2. **Listen** — to "Slow Fade" by Casting Crowns, and think about the implications of the lyrics.

3. **Care for a Plant** — Recall from your elementary school years that plants need sun, soil, and water to survive. Purchase a plant that needs to be watered often. Without water it will die. But when it is taken care of properly, it thrives. Let taking care of the plant be a reminder to you that you also need daily spiritual nourishment.

4. **Listen** — to "Shine On" by Needtobreathe. Then decide to shine brightly for Jesus Christ wherever you go.

Spending Time Alone with God

Monday: Psalm 20:4
May he give you the desire of your heart and make all your plans succeed.

Tuesday: Ephesians 6:10-17
Be strong in the Lord and in his mighty power. Put on the full armor of God, so that you can take your stand against the devil's schemes. For our struggle is not against flesh and blood, but against the rulers, against the authorities, against the powers of this dark world and against the spiritual forces of evil in the heavenly realms. Therefore put on the full armor of God, so that when the day of evil comes, you may be able to stand your ground, and after you have done everything, to stand. Stand firm then, with the belt of truth buckled around your waist, with the breastplate of righteousness in place, and with your feet fitted with the readiness that comes from the gospel of peace. In addition to all this, take up the shield of faith, with which you can extinguish all the flaming arrows of the evil one. Take the helmet of salvation and the sword of the Spirit, which is the word of God.

Wednesday: Isaiah 55:8-11
"My thoughts are not your thoughts, neither are your ways my ways," declares the Lord. "As the heavens are higher than the earth, so are my ways higher than your ways and my thoughts than your thoughts. As the rain and the snow come down from heaven, and do not return to it without watering the earth and making it bud and flourish, so that it yields seed for the sower and bread for the eater, so is my word that goes out from my mouth: It will not return to me empty, but will accomplish what I desire and achieve the purpose for which I sent it."

Thursday: Isaiah 30:21
Whether you turn to the right or to the left, your ears will hear a voice behind you, saying, "This is the way; walk in it."

Friday: Psalm 92:1-4
It is good to praise the Lord and make music to your name, O Most High, proclaiming your love in the morning and your faithfulness at night, to the music of the ten-stringed lyre and the melody of the harp. For you make me glad by your deeds, Lord; I sing for joy at what your hands have done.

Recommended Devotionals

Shining Through the Psalms, by Deborah Presnell

Streams in the Desert: 366 Daily Devotional Readings, by L.B. Cowman

Jesus Calling, by Sarah Young

My Utmost for His Highest, by Oswald Chambers

Radical Devotions for Girlfriends, available from Amazon.com

His Daily Bread, available online.

The Upper Room, available online.

End Notes

[1] Fredric Neuman, M.D. "Low Self-esteem. What Is It? What to Do About It" *Psychology Today*. April 14, 2013. psychologytoday.com/blog/fighting-fear/201304/low-self-esteem.

[2] https://www.npr.org/sections/krulwich/2012/09/17/161096233/which-is-greater-the-number-of-sand-grains-on-earth-or-stars-in-the-sky

[3] *KJV Online Dictionary*, The King James Bible Page. http://av1611.com/kjbp/kjv-dictionary/quiet.html

[4] Merriam-Webster Online Dictionary, copyright © 2015 by Merriam-Webster, Incorporated.

[5] Kost and Henshaw, "U.S. Teenage Pregnancies, Births and Abortions, 2010: National and State Trends by Age, Race and Ethnicity," 2014, New York: Guttmacher Institute

[6] Ibid.

[7] http://www.christianet.com/abortionfacts. Copyright© 1996-2015 ChristiaNet®.

[8] *Divine Moments,* Copyright © 2014. Published by Grace Publishing, Broken Arrow, Oklahoma.

[9] Macmillian Dictionary, © Macmillan Publishers Limited 2009–2015. http://www.macmillandictionary.com/us/dictionary/american/equip

[10] Charles Stanley, *In Touch Magazine,* InTouch Ministries, Atlanta Georgia; May 2013. Daily Devotions from *The Sermons of Charles Stanley* — Day 22, page 53.

Notes for Facilitator/Parent/Teacher

To Facilitator/Parent/Teacher

Although Christian morals and values are instilled in (and accepted by) our children when they are young, those views are not always deemed popular by their teenaged peers. This Bible study was born out of my joint desire with my daughter to be prepared for the struggles and drama associated with being a teenager.

I am an ordinary mom who believes the promises given by God in Jeremiah 33:3 — *Call to Me and I will answer you and show you mighty things you do not know.* — And Isaiah 41:10 — *Do not fear, I am with you; do not be afraid for I am your God. I will strengthen you: I will help you, I will hold on to you with my righteous right hand.* And that's just what He did. He showed me how to help my daughter be a light to others.

Teens experience many challenges in general, in school, and within various group settings. The electronic devices used by our teens make secular information readily available, often before they are emotionally ready for it. Some of what teens use, have access to, or witness include: iPads and iPhones, raunchy suggestive magazine articles, texting and sexting, Internet access, pornography, television, reality television shows, computer games, extreme violence in schools, social media, sexuality at every turn, and teen pregnancy being accepted and even encouraged.

Life is just hard. For parents and for teens. A teenaged girl's identity, when based on her understanding of who God says she is, will help determine her response, participation, and choices during difficult, confusing situations. Additionally, an understanding of God's purpose and presence in her life will lead her to boldly live with confidence and bring glory to God.

The topics this study covers are:

- How God sees you
- Fashion
- Modesty
- Inner beauty
- Guys
- Friendship
- Talents
- Gossip
- Exhaustion and stress
- Spending time with God

I designed this study to be used together for nine weeks, one chapter a week. There is no homework. I used a variety of Bible translations including: NKJV, NASB, NLT, ESV, NIV, and HCSB.

I recommend group sizes ranging in number from five to ten. The teens with whom I developed this study said they enjoyed the small group setting because they felt freer to discuss personal topics and share prayer requests.

My original intent was for parents to use this study at home with their 7th-12th grade daughters and their friends. But it also works well for church small groups, a Sunday School, or a retreat.

Pick a specific day and time to meet regularly, or choose meeting times from week to week based on the participants' schedules.

When your teens arrive, assign the verses listed for that chapter. (See pages 110-117.) That way they can be ready to read their verse(s) quickly at the appropriate time. This will save time and make the study go more smoothly and quickly. When using the charts on pages 16 and 77, it is not necessary for them to use the version of the Bible listed with the reference. The Scripture versions are similar and teens will be able to easily find the scripture that matches the reference.

Consider singing a few praise songs together. Girls at this age really enjoy music.

Each chapter will require 1½ to 2 hours to complete. *Optional Activities* are listed at the end of each chapter. A theme night such as Taco Night or a Banana Split Party makes the evening extra fun and memorable. The facilitator may choose to teach the chapter in her home during a slumber party, allowing for more flexibility with time.

Praying for Yourself and Each Other gives the teens a place to record each other's prayer requests. Allow a few minutes at the end of Chapter 1 to discuss prayer requests. Participation is not required but is encouraged. The leader can participate if necessary to get things rolling and make others feel comfortable. Discussing this confidently, yet with transparency, gives the teens a chance to pray, lift up, encourage, and support each other. Chapters 2-9 give the teens a place to record their personal prayer requests.

Writing their requests down draws attention to how God is working in their lives and answering their prayers.

Journaling and Doodling Your Thoughts and Feelings is designed to encourage each teen to think specifically about how the study applies to her. It can be completed as a wrap-up during the last five minutes, or individually at home. Lines are provided for participants to write their thoughts, but there is also space for visual learners who would prefer to draw a picture or illustrate their feelings.

The *Spending Time Alone with God* section is not required homework. It is meant to encourage a healthy habit of meeting with God each day. Because teens are busy and often on the run from one activity to the next, these scripture passages are short in length and are purposely chosen as encouragement for daily living. (The Scriptures for this purpose come from the NIV.)

Although the study was written for nine weeks, don't be surprised if the girls ask to continue meeting through the year for continued support, encouragement, and prayer time.

As previously mentioned, an optional way to teach this study is by organizing a retreat. In this case you can schedule an appropriate number of studies in a day, intertwined with activities, optional crafts, and meals. Check with your church for facilities you might be able to use at low or no cost.

After completing this Christ-centered Bible study, teens will be better equipped to live in the light of God's truth. My heartfelt desire is that our teens will be able to constructively deal with the issues that confront them on a daily basis and then live out Matthew 5:16:

> *Let your light shine before men in such a way that they may see your good works, and glorify your Father who is in heaven.* (NASB)

Chapter 1 Scriptures

- John 1:12
- Jeremiah 1:5
- Jeremiah 29:11
- Zechariah 2:8*b*
- Exodus 19:5
- Psalm 139:17-18*a*
- Psalm 40:5
- Ephesians 2:10
- Isaiah 43:1*b*
- Jeremiah 31:3
- Acts 10:35
- John 10:10
- Psalm 139:13-14
- Deuteronomy 23:5*b*

Chapter 2 Scriptures

- Proverbs 31:22
- 1 Peter 3:3-4
- Proverbs 11:22
- Proverbs 2:11
- 1 Corinthians 10:32
- Ephesians 5:3
- Colossians 3:5
- 1 Timothy 2:9-10

Chapter 3 Scriptures

- 1 Peter 3:3-4
- Colossians 3:12
- Colossians 3:8
- Matthew 23:26
- John 14:16-17
- 1 Corinthians 6:19-20
- Psalm 45:13

Chapter 4 Scriptures

- 2 Corinthians 6:14
- 1 Corinthians 6:18
- Ecclesiastes 3:1

Chapter 5 Scriptures

- James 3:5*b*-6
- James 3:3-4
- Proverbs 12:18
- James 1:26
- Psalm 39:1
- Ephesians 4:29
- Proverbs 16:28
- 1 Timothy 5:13
- Proverbs 15:28
- Proverbs 20:19
- Proverbs 11:13
- Proverbs 10:19
- Colossians 4:6
- Proverbs 15:1
- Proverbs 15:4
- Proverbs 16:24
- Matthew 12:34-35

Chapter 6 Scriptures

- Proverbs 27:17
- Proverbs 17:17
- Romans 12:15
- 1 Corinthians 15:33
- John 11:35
- John 11:36

Chapter 7 Scriptures

- 1 Peter 5:6-8
- John 10:10
- 1 Corinthians 14:33
- 2 Timothy 1:7
- Jeremiah 17:8
- Matthew 11:28
- 2 Corinthians 4:8-9
- James 1:2-4
- 1 Peter 1:6-7
- Matthew 7:24-25
- Philippians 4:13
- Proverbs 12:15
- Luke 1:37
- Jeremiah 32:17*b*
- Psalm 27:1
- Psalm 91:4
- Psalm 50:15
- Philippians 4:6
- Isaiah 30:21
- Jeremiah 33:3
- Psalm 25:4-5
- Psalm 32:8
- Isaiah 41:10
- Psalm 119:18
- Psalm 18:6
- John 14:13-14
- Mark 6:31

Chapter 8 Scriptures

- Psalm 20:4
- Genesis 37:5
- Genesis 37:28
- Genesis 41:14-15
- Hebrews 13:20-21
- 1 Corinthians 12:7
- 1 Peter 4:10

Chapter 9 Scriptures

- Psalm 1:2-3
- Galatians 5:22
- Hebrews 2:1
- James 4:8
- Psalm 50:14
- Psalm 50:23
- 2 Timothy 3:16-17
- Jeremiah 33:3
- 1 Peter 5:7
- Matthew 8:23-27
- Psalm 66:18
- Psalm 51:10
- James 1:5
- Psalm 119:18
- 1 John 4:4
- John 16:33

About the Author

Deborah Presnell, M.A.Ed., whose career has spanned more than three decades of teaching — from elementary school to higher education, where she trained future teachers — is a member of Gardner-Webb University's Gallery of Distinguished Alumni, a published author, national speaker, and Bible study teacher.

She is also a national spokesperson for Mukti Mission in India as she partners with Mukti Mission U.S. to bring hope, healing, and life to women and children of India.

Debbie is called to inspire women and feels honored when God allows her the opportunity to share at women's events about His faithfulness. For over twenty-five years, she has spoken at teacher conferences and universities where she shines the light on her favorite topic: "The Inspirational Classroom: A guide for teachers in all school environments." This will be the subject of an upcoming book.

Debbie's first book, *Shine! Radiating the Love of God — A Bible Study for Young Women in Middle School and High School*, is used in her popular Shine Camp. Her other books include *Shining Through the Psalms — A 150-Day Devotional Journey*, and *Shine On! — Biblical Principles for Radiant Living*. Her articles have been published in the *Divine Moments* series. She also blogs and brings inspirational messages on her Facebook page: ShineEveryDayNC.

Debbie and her husband, Alan, have three adult children and one granddaughter. She enjoys camping, riding her bike, helping coach a girl's running team, and she loves both the mountains and the beach.

When she's not busy writing or speaking, she serves as a substitute teacher in her local schools. But her best day is Sunday when her entire family gathers for lunch. Visit her website at www.debbiepresnell.com. Email her at debpres@yahoo.com for information about having her speak to your group.

www.ingramcontent.com/pod-product-compliance
Lightning Source LLC
Chambersburg PA
CBHW080445110426
42743CB00016B/3279